THE SEMANTIC DANCES

Bill McCullough

PublishAmerica
Baltimore

First printing

At the specific preference of the author, PublishAmerica allowed this work to remain exactly as the author intended, verbatim, without editorial input.

ISBN: 1-4241-6820-1
PUBLISHED BY PUBLISHAMERICA, LLLP
www.publishamerica.com
Baltimore

Printed in the United States of America

I dedicate this book of musings to my wife, Ruthie. Her common sense, computer expertise, and continual support via keeping me grounded has a great deal to do with the book you now hold in your hands.

To Dan,
With Wonder, Love,
Peace, & Joy!! :)

Bill [illegible]

I would be totally ungrateful if I did not acknowledge Barbara Lootens who opened my heart to poetry. I want to also thank each and every person I've encountered in my life, and I would finally and will always acknowledge the silence, the true author of these writings.

NOW

Bags
Blood bone bags
Move about, stop and shout about
Bags.
Engorged, enraged, enclosed,
Pound about, stop and ponder about
That which is without.
Never questioning the within
Or the between.
The between of thoughts and actions
Lovingly referred to as now…

Now I want to write about things
That cannot be said and are
Never ever thought about.

OUR TV GUIDE

In the beginning, God pulled up a chair, sat down, grabbed the remote, and turned on the TV. He surfed the channels, chortling out loud, enjoying and loving the crazy antics that only He could see on the tube.

We are His TV shows. His shows manifest the Alpha and the Omega. Being from and of Him, He abounds in self-esteem. As His actors, we painfully at times, but slowly, and yes Virginia, even surely advance toward our portion of the pie. The esteem lamp is ever lit for those who can liberate clicking device from deep within the hidden folds of the couch.

God looks out from all eyes and all senses to sense all eyes upon it all. Actor watches actors and actors watch actor for clues and cues about putting on the perfect show. Maybe even winning an award. Maybe even going to the award ceremony together—as one.

AFTER IT ALL

After it all

Back to being the tiny

being dancing on the marble.

After it all

the big stars and the bigger

stars still shine one on the other.

After it all

The many pains are chiseled from my eyes

pains I now see as not mine alone.

After it all

I know the sacred heart and I

know the bright shining infant.

After it all

The lowly manger reality continues to pulse

reality across the living universe.

After it all

The word of love

gently gathers all the marbles

together and silently trips away

Chuckling to Himself.

GRACING THE EDGE

From all reflected points

Dotting mirrors of dusty glass,

Scattered leaves explode

Through panes of memory.

Music in time; searching.

I'm a man no longer young

Sitting

Watching and listening.

My senses tuned to times of reflected points,

Tuned to many men

Reflected to form the whole,

To form a part,

To form but a reflected point.

"Hi Daddy, where are you?

Where are your reflected points?"

They say:

"A man must trust in something."

I trust the unconscious

    the undefined

    the unaccountable

    the unreliable

I trust reflections of nonsense

Sensually reflected non-sense.

(A life to walk through)

"Hi life!

What is your meaning?

Where is your reflected point?

Where is your Daddy?"

Dots,

Seuratish points scatter—

Flux

Energy/particle/energy/particle

Now and now and now and now

EPIPHANY!

I watch through glass, glassy-eyed

Reflecting/rejecting synaptic points

In my life.

Baggage, garbage, computer puke—

Unnecessary for light—

Make believe.

"Hang yer hat on it."

Creating myself in the salmon-swim.

Now reflecting points rub against reality

Creating the space. All

Unreal

Ultimately unreal

All ultimately unreal

From all reflected points.

SHALL WE?

It's a tango isn't it?

What arrangement do you hear?

Tree-framed clouds

Appearing as change

As the dance drives onward.

Staccato visuals

Rage

"Turn it down, Bobby!"

No, you turn it down.

It's from the inside out.

Tango or no

Arrangements pose as artifice

As vision changes not.

It's soup…those sounds,

That perspective of immature sight,

The violence of noise pathology,

Outward movements of control.

All, all must be supped,

Internalized

Made part of it all.

That is vanilla

That is a butterfly

That is silk

That is a tango.

THE REAL WORLD

Looking over his shoulder he watched his younger sister Tori awash in sweet play—he smiled autumnal as slants of pure light danced and sang with the beauty, the truth, and the wisdom of nature. Giggles and giggles peeled from reality following Tori round and round the isness of being. She ran toward him, arms wide to embrace, eyes wide to include, but he must and does turn away. The big yellow truck is waiting, and he must and does go with the others.

He is taken by the big yellow truck every day. He is taken to a building even his loving parents cannot free him from. In this building, he is told by big people what he must do and how he must do it. He is told when he may speak and when he may not. He is taught "important" things that Tori will also learn—things that have nothing to do with dancing light or the sound and sense of giggles.

Years pass. The big yellow truck still travels and delivers his and other bodies to buildings official. They learn what needs to be learned—what big people say needs to be learned.

There are rebellions, yes, from time to time when he feels the moment is ripe enough just to be a moment When he just wants to be—when his isness cries for expression. All to no avail.

Twelve years pass.

"What do you want to be?"

"I am what I want to be."

No, I mean what do you want to do with your life? What do you want to work at?"

"I don't know of any jobs I really want to do; my choices seem limited and arbitrary."

As they are talking and walking, they pass a dog chained to the middle of a yard. The dog is free. The dog is free to go only so far in any direction. But no farther. The dog strains at his collar; they walk by.

"You're just a dreamer. Get with the real world."

And he did. He got with the real world. He got a job; he got married and had children. He woke up every morning early, bolted breakfast and then out to, not a big yellow truck, but to his little yellow

V W Beetle—the people's car. He worked hard at his job—much overtime, and didn't see his family nearly as much as he wanted. But over the years he had developed a resignation to what the big people had always told him was the right thing to do. He was not so much happy as content. His family materially lacked for nothing. His company thrived and they needed him. He rarely saw Tori or heard giggles anymore.

But he did have his wall-sized TV with surround sound and 212 different channels. He and his family were entertained—he forgot his daily troubles and was in tune nightly with a vicarious life. And that was OK—he told himself he was happy. Big people on the screen taught him his values. Commercials taught him about his culture and on top of that kept his mind occupied with enough thoughts that he didn't have to labor and try to figure things out for himself. He told himself that life was good.

He grew old.

One day he was taking a walk—something he rarely did—when he saw a little girl who reminded him of somebody. As he approached, he saw that she was kneeling down beside a dog that had been tied to the middle of a yard. As he stood over them, the old man watched as the little girl set the dog free. Then looking up at him, she took his hand and began to giggle.

SERVING TIME

He never left the room.

The door was closed, the light on, the drapes drawn.

He sat in a room large enough for a small dresser, a chair, the aforementioned bed, and his thoughts.

He moved very little, lightly when he did with no thought surrendered to events beyond his immediate purview.

The drapes, now open, framed the bare trees of winter. Many with aged charm relaying intuitions of rest, dormancy, of life readying for renewal.

He heard their voices as he had for years. Vicariously he lived through their joys and tears. The woman, the young girl, and boy. He imagined them. Their forms and ways. He fed on their happiness and on their anger.

He never left the room.

He survived on thoughts of objective life. This was manna for his meager body. Though he was not a prisoner, he lived outwardly in pain and resisted the claim of an internal life.

He lived on. Through spring and fall his needs became less. Comfort and pain no longer fed his hunger. His senses declined.

The woman, the young girl, and the boy one day knocked on his door. He opened it and welcomed them in, and they never left the room.

INNOCENCE

I'm a happy little girl

I have blue fingernail polish on

My momdadandgrandmother are with me

We are in church

I love the bright stones

And motes of dust riding on holy light

I smile at my grandmother

We are in church…she is very sad

I smile at her and watch her closely

My face hers my face hers

I want her to be happy

Grandfather died last month…he is with God

Grandmother's only reality is loss

I'm a happy little girl

Tell me that I'm wrong

The president's in a heap of trouble

Iraq has chemical weapons

Terrorists threaten our safety

Millions on the planet are homeless

Greed abounds

Prejudice continues

Technology outraces humanity

God Himself is called into question

My tiny voice sings out the hymns

From my grandmother's songbook

I'm a happy little girl

Tell me that I'm wrong.

HIS LIFE

Exquisite particles of sweetness

Vaporize

"All time belongs to Him…" to

Him who is all particles

Of exquisite sweetness.

Vaporizing

Moving standing-still time

Into a new being.

Baby cries coalesce across ages

Across lines of words longer than

Forever.

Particle sweetness personified and

Dashed but not dead (an abstraction)

A notion like any other except

The liquified solidity of all.

Particular time recognizes itself

As itself.

Now as then the sweetness

Is the one exquisite taste and

Belongs to Him.

Rest in knowledge dark.

For it is all in all.

It is sweetness…it is His life.

FEAR

I await you

whose coming is here.

I await myself

whose coming is scattered

across the arching universe.

When shall I take courage?

Begin the dance?

Sing the one song?

When?

The train whistle blows,

and I am in that bed,

a child.

And I am safe,

and I am warm

and loved.

I hum softly the music

of the train.

I hum but do not sing.

My voice trembles, afraid of the song.

AN ETERNAL HAMMOCK

Long rows

        of palm trees

Monkeys

        at

    the top

    of each

        each having a monkey at the top

Monkeys

        each reaching across to his brother

Monkey

        forming   hammock

                an eternal

Two wooden men in a wooden car stop

get out walk woodenly to the back of

the wooden car…pause…then walk

(again woodenly) to the front door and

re-enter the wooden car never seeing

the monkeys but

dreaming of hammock

an eternal

leaping and of

Tigers in out water

an eternal

Beneath hammock

See: the wooden men leave

the wooden car

See: the tigers dash between the

comings and goings

of wooden extremes

To attack with

fond mauls &

sloppy licks

The wooden beards of

The wooden men who

Did not frolic in the water nor

See   hammock.

    an eternal

HENRIETTA'S UNAPPEALING PROBLEM

Henrietta Hippo had had it. She was 13 years old and just could not peel a banana correctly.

"I've had it," she squeaked in her high, whiney voice. "I just can't get it. I'm going to do something much easier—my homework. Don't try to stop me," she shouted to her poor mom.

Mother Hippo had tried and tried to teach her daughter the proper way to peel a banana, but Henrietta had never seemed to pick it up and now she was doing worse than ever.

Sitting in her small,cluttered room, Henrietta worked happily on her advanced calculus. Then her frustration and unhappiness reappeared when she heard her mom downstairs crying. She knew immediately that it was because of her and those stupid bananas. Her mom had always wanted her to be a prim and proper hippo, but Henrietta just knew she would never understand the correct way to peel a banana.

She thought about it for a while. She was always confusing the number of peels there were supposed to be. Was it 3 or 4? And did you start to peel from the bottom or the top? There were so many things to remember.

Suddenly she had an idea—maybe she could somehow connect banana peeling with math. Henrietta bent over her notebook and scribbled eagerly. No, that doesn't work, no, no, the remainder was too big.

Finally she had it! X=ab+c. She finally understood how to peel a banana. She jumped up and ran joyously to the stairs to tell her mom, who was still crying in the kitchen. Most unfortunately, on her way down, she slipped on a banana peel, fell, and broke every one of her fingers. She would never peel a banana again.

WHAT?

Feathers, glass

likable shine

Fumbling giggles of darkness.

Slippery reflections follow me down

Into the deepness of the darkness of my

Own giggling, likable pretensions

Reflecting sliding doors opening

Onto rooms of slant opinions

Leaked and bellowed.

Feathers float,

Glass cuts,

Light shines,

Reflecting likable nonentity.

CHASING TRUTH

They walked
And ran
And walked
And stumbled
And walked
And fell
And looked up
And saw you
And stood tall
And walked
And ran
And flew.

THE POURING

"Mom!"

"What is it, Cyril?"

"Mom, I don't have enough room."

"Did you brush your teeth?"

"Yes, Mom."

"Did you comb your hair? Did you…"

"Yes…yes…yes! Mom?

"Yes, darling."

"Mom, I can barely move around in here. What are we waiting for?"

"Why, Cyril darling, we're waiting for The Pouring!"

Cindy and Cyril Cereal were toasty flakes from the tribe of Oat. Cindy, of course, was the mom, and Cyril her young son. They, along with the rest of their clan, were happily settled in their box-like home on a super market shelf in Fort Wayne, Indiana. They were waiting to be chosen.

"I wish your father could see you now, Cyril. You're so handsome; he'd be very proud."

"Where is Dad?"

Cindy Cereal got super serious.

"Cyril, your father was such a good and loyal oat that he was taken by the pouring people many months ago."

"Will we ever see Daddy again?" asked Cyril.

"Soon after The Pouring all our oat relatives, including Daddy, will be together."

"Will we live in a box-home all scrunched together after The Pouring?"

"No, Cyril. Shortly after The Pouring, we will be living with many, many others in a place too wonderful to describe."

"Awesome!" shouted Cyril. "Mommy, we're moving!" Mommy, we're being shook all over the place-Mommy, is this an earthquake?"

"No, Cyril, hold on dear. Our journey is beginning."

And sure enough it was. During the next few days Cindy and Cyril were bounced and buffeted, shaken and shoved, thrown willy and darn near nilly till they almost gave up their dream of The Pouring.

"It's always darkest before the dawn," explained Cindy to a shaken Cyril. "Being cereal has never been easy, but our reward will be great."

All their travels had landed the toasty oat cereal folks in the home of Lila and Leroy Lamplighter. As brother and sister they lived just outside Fort Wayne in a burb called Spray. They were fine, upright young folks, and healthy too. They exercised and ate only the healthiest foods, which brings us back to Cindy and Cyril… doesn't it? Yep.

One gray morning when almost all the oat family had experienced The Pouring, Cindy woke Cyril.

"It's time! It's time!"

Cyril hopped right to it. Both he and Cindy were already ready when they heard the sound which had been talked about with great reverence by the oat elders—it was The Rustling.

"Are you ready, Cyril?"

"I'm ready, Mommy!"

And so they were poured. But hold on just a minute. Look there…no, not in the beautiful porcelain cereal bowl. Down under the table on the greenish beige linoleum floor. Those two spots. Those two spots are not really spots but instead…I'm afraid so. It's Cindy and Cyril Cereal. They missed the bowl.

Days passed. Cindy could barely keep up her motherly confidence. As a week dragged by, it was all she could do to make Cyril and herself presentable. Hair combed, teeth brushed, all that stuff. Not to mention how helpless they felt almost being stepped on.

One afternoon Cyril escaped a most horrible fate. He was almost licked up by Larry, Lila and Leroy Lamplighter's lizard.

However, that very same evening Leroy said to Lila, "Ya know Lila, I'm hungry. We got any more of those delicious toasty oats?"

"I think just a few," replied Lila.

So Larry lumbered from the living room, turned the kitchen light on, spied the box and...well you know what he did? He poured. And as he poured he peered off to his lower right, right by the fridge. Right where Larry (remember Larry?) had, in an attempted lick, scooted Cindy and Cyril to the far corner.

On his feet quicker than...oh, almost anything...Leroy ran to the corner, grabbed the oatsome two, checked them for cleanliness, and plopped them into the aforementioned porcelain cereal bowl.

As Leroy nourished himself, which was only proper, he couldn't hear the tiny voices of joy. But I could, and it sounded like this.

"Mommy, Mommy it's The Pouring!"

"Yes, Cyril, yes it is. Isn't it wonderful?"

"Oh, Mommy yes! What happens next?"

"I don't know, Cyril I really don't know."

COLORINGS

Stillborn thoughts

One step ahead of…

Insanity.

Is truth beauty, beauty truth?

Definitions of moments

Brought to fruition

And left free to flee

Unarmed back into black

Holes of incomprehension.

"Follow me down," they cry.

"Come with me," they scream.

Urging me incessantly,

Insistently toward what?

Where is yesterday, a moment ago?

What can be said of reality?

I hear the poets of old-

Keats Beethoven Blake.

I see visions of light

Where truth and beauty rule

In a kingdom where the masters play

Unconcerned.

Truth and beauty

With open eyes

Walk next to my moments,

Flash a smile,

And briefly I know the kingdom.

I am not allowed to stay…

Not yet.

I will wait; I will watch,

And I will try not to think too much.

STAR DOG

Star Dog, electric smile,

Attempting tricks that are beyond me.

To make me more, I would understand you

And be not more but less.

The reflection, I internalize

And make my own.

In my own eyes I grow,

And in my own eyes the reflection is clear.

Star Dog, mansions of light,

The view is true from my imprinted beliefs.

Beliefs, Star Dog, not in your ken.

They are but shadows of ash.

They are dropped from a floorless ceiling.

Sightless, clueless, Star Dog, I walk the feelings

Of almost despair.

But because I address you,

Because you have nodded in my direction,

Because I keep coming back for less than more,

You laugh and I know you.

And I know you are.

And I know you are real.

TILT

I started,

awakened by the man in the radio

saying that the moon was in the wrong place.

It was here and it should be here.

Back to sleep, perchance to dream.

Forget it!

What did this mean?

Is it really true?

I ran to my window, threw up the sash.

The moon on the thigh of the new fallen snow…

It was true!

Dammit! Dammit! Dammit! Tomorrow was Saturday!

Maybe…maybe it didn't make any difference.

Turn on the TV

"We're experiencing technical difficulties because the moon

is in the wrong place…

It is here and it should be here.

Please stand by; men with lassos and big long sticks are trying

to re-position the moon."

I didn't believe that,

and I don't expect you to believe it either.

But then it's all a dream.

We're both sleeping.

In your dream, you're reading my poem.

And in my dream I'm writing it.

I'm only a line ahead of you.

If I wake up first you'll have no more to read.

But you…you dream on;

you really have no choice.

I started,

awakened by the man in the radio…

TREE

She comes from my dreams

trailing closeness

to stand consciously straight

and naked to the bark.

Ever reaching toward surrender

through glooms of acquisition.

Again straight,

she exchanges her life for mine.

Then proudly rises

exquisite in my line of vision,

lovely in her all.

JEN TO MICKEY

They are reeled in, one and then the rest. Days upon end and moments dull as they are repeated. I am here in this place/ time again…now and now. Once in awhile what we live for occurs. We are alive for the epiphanies which can be had via an open heart. A child's smile and the play of little girls on tree swings. Crisp Autumn sunsets, sky laced with majesty and color, chill smell of burning leaves. Long wonder-filled letters from old friends. A good book. Knowledge of beauty, the formless formed to intimate eternal, creative Aliveness. Music you listen to and hear God singing again and again, always new…surprising the moment, sending the pastfuture fleeing in mediocrity and shame.

Live your life well, as I know you will. Remember the moment. We are born for and will die into the moment to live as the flame shed of the ash.

MICKEY TO JEN (PART 1)

We live so far away from each other, all of us. Even though we inhabit the same relative space, we are caught up in our own thoughts, hopes, dreams, fears. Our world views are similar only because we have eaten the gruel that the powerful of our culture have dished up. Our bellies full, we are content with place and time and our role in it. We walk about in our own coolness, we are the bomb, we know the dance and we tell those who can't follow the steps to get off the dance floor. We are cruisin'. We are our own God. We are, in spite of all the role-playing and the costumes, alone. We need a hug.

You offered to share a hug with me. How can I not care for you? Unlike most of us, caught up in our own stuff, you reached out to let another into your life, and you continue to do so. How can I not care for you?

The biggest sin, the greatest danger to us as a people, as individuals is to close ourselves off from each other. However, we do it time and time again. It's a reflex action whenever someone gets too close. Close enough to know our real selves—not the façade, not our cool selves, our real selves. The selves that come from/with love; these selves are fragile and these selves are too smart to dance in this world's ballroom.

We must begin to realize that to swallow our culture whole leaves no room for our real selves. It's like pretending—it's like going to sleep and dreaming. Most people never wake up.

I've seen you awake. I've seen the shine of your smile. I've read the words you've shared with me. I know by these and many other intangible things that you care for me. You see the sometimes buried truth in me that connects with the truth in you. How can I not care for you?

CARLOS

Blips of you

Crackle down my body

Toward and

Quickly away

From memories that have been

from birth

A cause of paradoxical circumstances.

Explaining nothing of anything

By being then or

Being now

only trying

To make out of nothing

Anything I can

Keep your feeling

Close to what I call,

"The place where I keep all the things

That I love most in the world." If

You don't know

now

then you'll never know—

But

since they changed the furniture

I believe

You can catch

The next train

Due in and

to

the fact that

The chair is no longer

In front of the door and

The mini-window

remains only

To occasion wet glances at

Mr. Williams' crimson carrier of waste.

THE LEGEND OF LANDO COFFEY

Urp, the kid, Terwilliger Goss, and the tightrope, Lily, who owlishly resembled coffee and indeed had lived in Fantasy with no other desire than to milk into the sediment remains of the bean.

Characters,

Actors of the noblest ardor, pilgrims of virginal descent, babes incarnate, driven away in Goss' opening-lined Edsel.

(Nate, not knowing, never knew)

Cliffs and savage eyes, verdant mists of hemorrhoidal applica's, thunderous savage ego, breast beating, and eating gardens all.

Till blood red arose in their eyes, till blood blue formed their anger.

Followed closely by the handing out of roles with lines to be learned, parts to be played. Anger subsided, I's counted seven up to and including Nate's dismissal.

Goss now up in the top of the first suffered a recall of his Ed and spitefully approached Omega, spitting tales of bitchiness and self delusion though his mark on the proceedings nonetheless was not unimportant…at least to Terwilliger, ah Terwilliger, straight "A" teeth smiled past gums of insufficient strength, even though being a Catholic he used them, to no avail, fathering fourteen lemon-colored Dumbo-eared, watery-eyed lemmings.

All of whom rushed over aforementioned cliff whispering something about their duty.

Howdy Urp, formerly formed formless.

As a disciple of Nate's car and luckily to be addled by flaxen-headed misses to walk like a cracker,Urp spermed the soft cuddilys till OK Corral time. This time the end was different.

You guessed it.

But then back to the kid bored to death then to Lily walking over red hot coals on a cool April eve (about 6 o'clock). She surprisingly, though unmistakably, squatted. The kid, his karmal-covered apple kicking, biting, choking, and crying. A damn whore Eve freaked his head. Getting over same by stable stench, the kid, his mom Lil, both walked the tightrope of molecular banging until finally with hammers and nails he got hung up on his own idea and sent a telegram to his daddy Lando Coffey and the above, boys and girls, is the stuff legends are made of.

MISTER SIX

Mister six touches the sky

...listening for death

While visiting Glamorous Ladies of Wrestling

or (...). No difference

when nobody has time.

Just something to do

while waiting in line.

Mister six wanders his mind

...tasting the night

(as worms continue to gnaw his neck)

after the fall. The discontent

beneath the stars.

Mister six watches blank stares

...licking the water

he reaches for the black star,

lances a vein

and awaits the winter

before the tube.

NEVER GROW OLD

Oh my oh my I

Remember how he'd

Shine

And how crystal

Tears

Scarred his cheeks

How exquisite his

Misery.

Oh my oh my I

Remember sparks

Flying from his fingers

And intervals of

Creamy silence

How transforming his

Glory.

Oh my oh my I

Remember childhood's

Joy

Wrapped in age old

Body

In anticipation of

Commencement.

Oh my oh my I

Remember love-rays

In the new,

Forever tuned to,

Chords

Announcing the final

Vision.

Oh my oh my I

Remember death

Falling in love

The unification of the

Spheres

Completed in

A young girl's smile.

EYES CLOSED

An old man with satin boots

A middle-aged woman who sells nails

Three businessmen on their way to LA

A child not yet fully conceived

Manufacturers of filth

A dwarf with one eye

Two mothers joined by folly

Presidents of bottling companies

The child we all once were

Golden-haired princesses from Siam

Astronauts home from the moon

Drunkards in out of the rain

Babies selling mascara from cribs

Neighbors to whom you never speak

Wonderful ladies whom you've touched

Believers in all assorted sordid dreams

Tiny people too timid to be

Revolutionaries fresh from a trip

A black man who dreams of tigers

Grandmothers who refuse to die

A single cigar swallower

Mike Wallace's secretary's mother-in-law

A waif-like girl whose eyes begged more

And you

        and I

We all

        all of us

Stood around it

                wondering

Stood around it

                pondering

Stood around it

                but never once

Asked

                what it was.

ORALITY: ONCE AND ALWAYS

Red

Well read and

understanding

curved surfaces crying to be covered

with accents. Accent dancing.

Struggling. Up and down

came after

without tea but with

a sense of fresh mintness

lending gustatory sanction

to

tactile rational.

Her mouth swollen, paused

(streaming tears of light from

the always-cast textural grins

upon the tilt of your own

particular slant on reality.)

Then

changed again and again and again.

Beginnings remembered, video-taped,

and replayed for God.

Red

is partially driven from play,

deposited in handy corner (never worked but always applying)

has retired w/pension and

Animal juices

spill

through

ways, sin-free.

Swollen twosome, delightful

In pellucid linen meet

And decide

on tea after all. (And all that, til now, never was.)

Atomic whispers, knowing glances

integrate

unify

shock

til our mantra pays without tip

(later) but

          aways

taking it (all) in (its) now

we become what we are!

We become what we are…

The cat sits knowingly;

The dog remembers a bone,

but is embarrassed and does his dog-embarrassed eyes.

(We are)…now the tip

eternally begotten of the Father

Son-like

Accepting the rush.

JASON PURRS

My name is Jason Purrs. I tell you this straight out so that you don't mistake me for someone else. Nobody would but you might because, and only because, you don't know me yet. Nobody else would mistake me for someone else because they know me. All the theys, they know me. You'll see.

I'm at school…actually outside school waiting for my father to pick me up in his old truck. His old truck. If I drove, had my license, I might say our old truck. Might. But it is old; it is his, and I'm waiting.

People around me, students, boys and girls, are either driving, walking, or running to drive or be driven by friends—boys with girls, boys with boys, girls with boys, girls with girls—you get the picture. And so do I. I'm not stupid. I do look rather stupid, let's face it (but I'm not) waiting for my old father to drive me home from school in his old truck.

Usually I see him first, and I begin to walk towards the old truck. Then he sees me and we meet somewhere between the jocks and the cheerleaders. I watch my feet as I walk. They always look the same, my feet, as do I in my baggy parochial school uniform—pants and shirt. Conformity is everything. Exterior conformity saves me from expecting to be stared at. I watch my feet conform to the same heavy-footed pattern that leads me every day after school to my father's old truck.

I am not smiling. There are those around me who smile as my feet and eyes avoid them. They are not serious people. They, (remember they? Those who know me?) are smiling, and some even have the audacity to laugh in rhythm with their non-conforming bodies. My savior body conforms. Inside my baggy clothes, my baggy body follows my feet, watched by my eyes till I get to my un-smiling father's old truck.

He's drunk, as usual. I throw my book bag in ahead of me. He stares as I climb into the cab next to him. He doesn't speak. We don't speak. Rarely. He manages to avoid smashing smiling bones frolicking in and out of shiny cars and new trucks till at last on the main drag we settle in to our own brand of fog. I notice my shoe is untied. Bending through my father's fog, blue (he smokes); I bang my head on the open glove compartment which is filled with fishing equipment, lures, stuff. "God dammit!" I mutter under my breath.

My father asks what God has to do with it. I make a disgusted grimace-looking face and turn to look out the nicotine-coated window. He laughs till he coughs up phlegm and spits it into a coffee can filled with mucus and cigarette butts.

It is nearly twilight, for it is nearly Winter. He and I continue our parts in the world's play. Numb, yet relentless, we no longer hear the applause.

OLD LOVERS

Little old raisin ladies with stockings rolled half past three in the heat of the little old raisin men stumble past stubble stuffing stuff of their very own reflections, straining to catch the next breath Thursday, July 23 will dole their way. With lizard-like longing for the sleek young cats with paws and furry cough balls they are tolerated for the opposites they give birth and lend credence to.

She was quite quaint and quiet, my raisin lady was and had been so since she at an early age was touched once, but only once, let out to let another in and quickly back again for she had been afraid and was to this day, whenever it may appear, in her tea room her lizard friend's room or on the park bench in the world room where she sat this day whenever it may appear.

Silently sliding stained glassy-eyed through this moment of his terminal existence to look down but back again at the white poodle racing the right way toward a wrong way freeway from a wrong way world…just watching, mouth agape, spewing Mail Pouch down his tablecloth mind and being unable to change the poodle's course nor his own. Looking down and back no more, my raisin man, with more grace than he possessed appeared in the leading role of my raisin lady's movie.

The sooner our happiness together begins, the longer it will last...crinolins and marshmallow dreams, grass that was blue and skies that were green. The times our stomachs hurt to be so much in love, and the times our stomachs hurt to be so much alone. Peach faces, milk bodies and to open our arms was to embrace the world. Some say we ran before we walked, some say we never even knew how to walk...and to this day, some say marshmallow dreams.

In the world room they sat, side by side, late in the day of their years, whenever it may appear and mourned one way, wrong way, so-called freeways, though none were nor ever were nor ever would be. Games were played and paid for with heart-shaped tokens, worn thin now by many changes of script, character, and direction of this epic drama.

They were the warm summer, orange blossom odor days...but were not. They were the marshmallow dreams reveled in total abandon…but still they were not. They were the quiet nights, grass dewed thundering, wanting, needing hearts that urged love through the world's body…but even now, more than then, they were not.

The sooner our happiness together begins, the longer it will last.

My raisin man and raisin lady, with but a brief remembering glance, arose from the park bench in the world room and once again went their separate ways.

GETHSEMANI

There is a boy here

who should not go unmentioned.

He smiles at me

and I am afraid,

threatened somehow.

His gentle face,

his long pony tail seriously silent,

his easy grace serene.

What does he want?

I hope to not see him again

yet fear that I will not.

Imaginings.

What is God's one true mind?

And what is only of my making?

I've come to doubt my reliance

on and my accountability toward the Real.

Still I walk that razor's edge,

and fancy this Buddha-faced boy

but a lower case reality

and not the Christ that chases me

into each moment.

Only now

I look him in the eye.

He is beautiful.

I will follow him out of the garden.

HOLICS OF CHOCOLATE

Like climbing stairs. Like putting one foot in front of the other. Like being without enough breath. Like, "What's up here anyway?"

Faces and bodies

Ed, you, and cation

The three of you

(It was then that you and Lady Aberlin occupied space together. It was simple and lovely. It was a dream.) But tumbling ignorance from the nutrient orifice fit itself into gaudy imitations, adjusted to levels of disinterest, and more often than not, became the real dream.

Yes, you, then.

Some of it remains. Yes, you—memories even when spoken to never admit complicity. Even when pleaded with, hold you to be the blame. Even when silent, race through your veins—burning never quite enough to be forgotten, to be other than who you are.

You and the girl and both of you together, trinity, epiphany, atonement. Simple and lovely. It didn't last; it continues.

EDEN

Driving a more than familiar highway,

A human rut sat

Behind a wheel.

(Personified hyperbolic symbolism, to be sure)

But, to be sure

The inability to be so

Had precipitated its fall.

In the autumn of its years

The aforementioned,

In the midst of a drive,

Pulled to the side of the road.

Off then, and out from

Behind a wheel

In one motion.

But, to be sure

It was the lack of motion

That started it all.

Epiphanies of sun

Slanting and dazzling its eyes. Stillness

(Masquerading as arrested moments) disporting Itself,

Explored the creature's naked body.

For although it was clothed

In commerce

In blood—political and greedy—

These trappings held no power

Over this innocent

Who was not in want

Of momentary grace.

Stepping, spongy and green,

Over fully-lived flashes of fire

Unaware of the universal pattern

Tick and tock

The creature saw one of its own.

It had never seen one before.

(Replicants of course,

Coarse with hair and the like.)

But now, spending but a beat

In the other's eye,

Its heart was spoken to

And spoke.

"I just stopped. I should be home now,

But I've been there and everywhere. So

I just stopped."

"I'm glad you did. Just a bit ago

I stood on a chair; I looked at God

And was not afraid."

"Is He tall?"

"He is. And everything else too."

The creature began to feel the pull of routine,

Began to think of moving.

"Come with me," it said.

"Oh, I couldn't…they need me…

My family. They love me."

"They love you? You who stand on chairs

And measure God?"

"I…I never told them. Where would we go?"

"Nowhere. There is nowhere to go."

"Yes, I see…yes,

I will go with you."

The sun, at this time,

Grew straight and dull.

Arrested moments ran free

And recognized the creatures' naked bodies.

The roads moved; the ticks tocked.

The creatures ducked for cover

Into a land they must share again

With strangers.

Somewhere, bathed in patience,

A chair waits.

LITTLE WONDER THING

What is truly happening little wonder thing?

Have we perverted epiphanies?

Or can we honestly take a position at all?

And what about this "we"?

Little wonder thing

Reveal to we our home.

Give we the courage

To tear up the map of senses,

Give we the tender vulnerability

To shed the blanket of fear.

Give thyself to we little wonder thing.

We try so hard to avoid thee,

But we love thee in moments.

We love thee in confusion little wonder thing

We love thee when love has lost all meaning,

When thoughts no longer come,

When all the answers are questioned,

When ecstasy is empty,

When convention is crippled and bloody,

When God has finally died.

BEAUTY

Think of the most beautiful person you have ever seen. Think of the exact moment you looked into his or her eyes, and for a fleeting second you were paralyzed; you couldn't take your eyes off that vision. You stared, frozen in time, caught in that instant of beauty. Now imagine that identical beauty radiating from every single thing in the entire universe: every rock, every plant, every animal, every cloud, every object—even garbage dumps and broken dreams—every single one of them emitting that beauty. You are quietly frozen by the gentle beauty of everything that arises around you. You are released from grasping, released from avoidance, released from time, released altogether into the eye of spirit, where you contemplate the unending beauty of the art that is the entire world.

That all-pervading Beauty is not an exercise in creative imagination. It is the actual structure of the universe. That all-pervading Beauty is in truth the very nature of the cosmos right now. It is not something you have to imagine because it is the actual structure of perception in all domains. If you remain in the eye of spirit, every object is an object of radiant Beauty. If the doors of perception are clean, the entire cosmos is your lost and found Beloved, the original face of primordial Beauty, forever, and forever, and endlessly forever. And in the face of that stunning Beauty, you will completely swoon into your own death, never to be seen or heard from again, except on those tender nights when the wind gently blows through hills and mountains quietly calling your own name.

THAT PLACE

The wind tore the skin from my

Face

In conjunction with the sun, it

Worked

Till I was worn and away

Then scattered into everything.

I was lost and afraid.

I had no anchor, no thought to stand for

Or against.

There was no me.

I was lost and afraid.

All that was not me became physically ill.

With no concepts, my mind became a sobbing child.

I struggled to recall familiar themes,

Things I had loved: music, literature, beauty.

Where was the land of grace and dignity?

Nothing

Nothing really does mean…nothing.

No thing in the one song.

No thing in the uni verse.

Then I was not afraid.

There was no thing to be afraid of.

A subtle shift,

The sparkle seen

Although not seen, nor sound nearly heard

Terminal senses

Strip,

Metamorphosis flashes

Infinity.

And I was song and verse;

I was beauty and truth.

I was I am.

A child handing me a flower

Is myself.

Tears stream from my being;

I hear familiar voices.

"Are you alright?"

What can I say?

THREE HAIKU

Three birds on a wire

Against the pale blue sky, now

Dreaming of heaven.

Night sounds in my mind

Tardy sandman late for work

I stare at the rain.

Shadows on the snow

Sun is shining mightily

On our way to spring.

LICK YER LIPS

The cows are standing on the ice. The farmer is eating ice cream. His name is Ed. Farmer Ed also has chickens. Only one of Farmer Ed's chickens likes ice cream; his name is Seymour. Seymour likes strawberry ice cream. Strawberries and cream are a favorite of Ed's. The cows are standing on the sun. The farmer is smiling the sun upon all that he sees. The sun's name is Vito. Vito smiles as the farmer sees his farm. The cows are standing on silence. The farmer is talking the roots of language, while Seymour and Vito party in the yard—with the sun and the chickens eating ice with cream and strawberries... oh, liberation...oh, knee-slapping jubilation...oh, slants of cosmic giggles.

BEFORE THE ALTAR

Ether types

Illicit unions

Naked mimes

White mouthings

Tawny long-legged

Sattvic dancers

Style conscious moods

Little loving girls

Besmeared reflections

Counterfeit echoes

Out of tune.

A small woman was standing in the doorway

there was a little woman standing in the doorway

there was a tiny

woman with a scarf

standing in the doorway there was a woman with a scarf

around her head

standing in the doorway with a scarf around her head

a woman stood watching

three horses standing dead

still

standing dead still

dead still

three horses

standing dead still.

Jackie call the horses

Jackie black Jackie black black Jackie black black black Jackie

Jackie

call the horses.

Nine year old Jackie nine year old eyes

Nine year old black Jackie nine year old thighs

nine year old eyes

nine year old thighs

Jackie call the horses

I Am

that one

who watches nine year old eyes

who watches nine year old thighs

Young legs hanging from rooftops

legs hanging from rooftops staring

from rooftops at three dead still horses

Jackie

call the horses.

I Am

that one

who watches Jackie the woman the legs the horses

watches Jackie the woman the legs watches Jackie the woman

watches Jackie

nine year old Jackie

call the horses

three

dead still horses

dead

still horses three

still

dead horses three

horses

dead still.

Jackie call the horses nine year old Jackie call the horses

black Jackie

Jackie.

DROP THE ASH

He has lived, is living, a life of pretense. But then isn't that all we are given to live? (to be continued) or not to be continued. That in modern life, dear Hamlet, is the only question.

Not, however, a continuing as opposed to an ending, but to another continuing.

Past the pretense.

Out beyond the stars.

Inward toward the fire.

To allow it to burn far past the make believe which has seemed to serve him well.

To burn the shame and the sham,

the vitriol and the vanity,

and arrive.

And in motions of frolic and delight, play in fields of childhood.

TINY'S TIME

Home smells, home time, out of time time, in time smells, rhythm method, time smells smelly time, dancing on the 69th indentation 13 down Lincolns, Tiny addressed the house. Lightly chuckling to himself of a little known time when a dime was a dime and not a martyr to coin johns. John's time and my time in search of Tiny. To say he had a time admitted miniature voice prints who became quite annoyed. Tiny's time (I continue) vainly apologizes for itself pointing at 69x13 Lincoln, on the corner covered with wino phlegm and bits of toback making time taking time, thinking of smelling home and fleetingly doing time. Quietly now we approach to reproach the egg-shaped manner of his delivery. Poached, not coached to slide down gaily to awaiting eternal judges of Eydie-dom. Time rolled Tiny six and seven and was ready to elfinly speak of spots of yellow snow children would gorge into time capsuled muffin-like wraps… when a taste, only a tad, of silver multiformed time settled on the right side of Tiny's left nostril, causing Tiny's time to come and gravely disappointing the squatting multitude.

THE QUEST

Vision

clothed only in innocence

and light

burning from the frame

into my memories

far past the moment.

Now

and always pubescent

now

and always now.

In this precious instant

she moves slightly slowly silently

as I fly past toward

epiphanies that pale.

And I fly past again, always

and now and again,

now.

FOR YOUR CONSIDERATON

Man is created (present tense) in the image of God. However, man is a material being, and God is a spiritual being. What to think? What to do? Not to worry. God is the Alpha and the Omega, All that is. God does not fill the universe; God is the universe. The universe is composed of atoms. Material: atoms bunched together, imprisoned, seemingly separate from each other. Spiritual: atoms free, playing, connecting one to another and to all. Man is being created in the spiritual image of God. Since God's "real" image is spiritual; man's "real" image is spiritual.

When, however it happened, (we'll let quantum physics and the philosophers figure that one out) God put on flesh, He became us in the physical, bunched together form, as well as continuing to be us in the spiritual form, free. God, the man Jesus, did what He did and said what He said as an indication to all physical/spiritual beings of what we all could/should do in order to realize "heaven", in order to understand the truth of the mystery, in order to understand who we really are.

Spirit, of course, being beyond space/time (a relative man-made function of this material plane) is always present everywhere. God's reality, our spiritual image is being created in every moment, in every place. God, then, becomes man to reveal to us our identity and our home.

The question arises, why are we all not, 2000 years later, snuggly tucked into the wonder of God's bed? The answer is that most of us hearing God's voice, harden our hearts. He knocks at our door; we do not answer. We are afraid. We are afraid because if we open our door and soften our hearts and nobody's there, we have nothing. We are not brave enough to love, not brave enough to re-cognize fellow atoms as part of All That Is, as ourselves. We are too self-absorbed to have that faith and to empty ourselves to find out who we really are. So we fill ourselves with vicarious lives: our jobs our responsibilities, our gods.

One man went all the way. He tells (present tense) the eternal truth in the now of every moment, in the here of every place. If we have eyes, we can see; if we have ears, we can hear. We need only attend the moments of our lives to know that as we are seeing and being rightly seen, we are the image of God. Jesus is saying, "See, I am man just like you, and you are God just like me."

NIKKI AND THE SERPENT

You would not have wanted to know
anything about her life
before she took her pleasure
with the serpent.
Even I did not want to know her then.
(But quite often I did see her with Amber.)
It was not that she lacked a certain
indiscriminate style.
No. It was more than that.
Maybe it was the cutting boys
who when with her, like Zimmy
were tangled and powdered in blue
singing and dancing,
Nichole Sharra du Perault.

Even though he had done volunteer work
for the Dalai Lama in the last election,

he was considered eccentric.

He would work far into the night

with and oftimes without his daughter Nikki.

One night refusing to live in anyone else's world

he dreamed of the gun, the razor, the poison.

He dreamed of Nikki and the serpent

locked between spaces

where air was remembered, but only.

And only by the cutting boys.

To get in was to enlighten the darkness.

To get out was easily as difficult.

Before/Between/After

The ins and outs,

The glory lived

in ecstasy and demise.

Until Nikki and the serpent

effected the change.

ADVERBIAL MYSTERIES

I looked straight at him and I said…I said, "I'm lookin' fer Tiny ed."

He answered right up. "You'll find Tiny ed in a manila envelope."

I figured I needed to do some figurin' so I went with haste to my figurin' foyer. In the corner.

He followed me over, spit in my ear and said the following, "It seems mighty bizarre."

Wiping the abusive spittle that had cascaded onto my beard, I mentioned that perhaps he should refrain from speaking of my wife's unmentionables. He thought that was rather humorous so handing me an armful of mail and with a baleful look in one of his eyes he asked me three questions: Would I post them? Am I sincere in my search for Tiny ed?

I answered, "Yep," and "Yep," and…

Walking slowly in the direction of the post office, I ran into Pendrecki (neither one of us was hurt) a man who possessed the knowledge of the ages, and I asked him, "Pendrecki, how old is Tiny ed?"

Before he could answer, his dog, Millard Fillmore, asked me about my drinking preferences and if I had a favorite part of speech.

Just about that time I was surprised by a sudden and violent shiver coming directly from somewhere within the mountain of mail I was transporting. Before I could attend to or even wonder about, a long forgotten 60's sound swam through my brain. I whirled (a remembered move from childhood ballet classes) and stared into the eyes of Millard's sister Janis and her promoter, Graham. Janis was top-dog in the school for the ominously challenged. "One eye must always be alert." sang Janis in her best Bessie Smith voice.

I agreed.

She wouldn't let me out of her sight. "Well, answer my brother."

"Any old beer and yes." I agreed again and then implored her to let me be on my way, and she did.

Millard Fillmore excused himself, and Pendrecki said, rather casually I thought, that he was off to the Middle Ages.

So I also went off with my armful of shivering mail toward the post office. By the way, if you don't know that Tiny ed is in the manila envelope I'm carrying, you're not paying close enough attention.

When I got to the post office, I was met by this big fat woman who screamed, "I do declare…now you."

I said, "What?" Not knowing whether I was to declare or scream, I screamed my declaration that in point of fact I didn't know what I was declaring…or screaming for that matter.

It was then that the big fat woman suggested that we should open the manila envelope. Well, we did and out popped Tiny ed.

Surprised? Let's go talk to him. Shall we?

Tiny ed was, as might be expected, happy to be unbound, and as we settled in, he told us a story that would change all of our lives for the next twenty minutes or so.

"I'm off," he said, "in pursuit of justice, grace, and dignity for all mankind. I've recently become aware that life is not as it seems." By now a multitude had gathered, and we all gasped. Tiny ed continued. "Yes, it's true. The forces of symbol have forced themselves upon our collective consciousness and now men, women, and tiny babies live but do not live. The cacophony of clatter cascades cunningly through our minds and dances in tune with the dread tripper vac. Yes, it's true. I am on a mission to reverse man's fate, to awaken him from clutterdom and cacophs. And now, by your leave, taking up my thimble filled to the brim with mango madness Snapple and the adverb "quietly" I must begin."

Now sadly, the only reason I am here to tell this woeful tale and you are here to hear it is that just as Tiny ed turned to depart, he tripped, spilled his mango madness Snapple, and made such a terrible racket that his adverb fled…quietly.

Have a nice life.

Have a very nice life.

WHAT (PART 2)

"Men that look like trees walking" past notions

of desire. Passed out and in upon the times they

dream themselves to be. "Have you ever seen a dream

walking?" I have and dancing too, past men desiring

to look like the notion, only the notion, of trees dreaming

of walking men dreaming of dancing.

SNOW

Movement,

Between the now of then,

Slants through the darkness

Whispering love in a voice that imagines

The real, the obvious. Comfort and warmth

Smile and sing

(goosebumps beckoned by beyond)

And sing disguised as whistle sad and shrill

And solemn.

Snuggle.

Outside frigid faeries frolic in crystal white gowns,

Tongue-catching God's own silence…till from

Within this dream voices human filter softly

Into consciousness promising warmth, safety,

And security.

He is a gentle giant;

She is whom he has chosen.

    This place, time's distance

Shelters dreams

Strokes memories

Arouses sad and

Joyful tears. But

    Then, then as before, (and now) flakes from the darkness

    Illumine lounging beings angelic romping

    And rollicking.

    Till in a sudden shift, a puff,

    A calm becomes the all,

    And our minds meet, recognize, and revel

    In the silent snow of truth kissing white

    Mounds of being.

    I am taken, as always,

    Between the now of then, through the

    Darkness…whispering and listening.

GOING HOME

And then he began to think—

"Beyond the sheer curtains, reflecting sunlight slant off the yellow houses, off green leaves, framed as eternity, beckoning unwittingly, with no motive, the contemplative heart."

He thought—

"This coffee tastes good, the chair comfortable, and my prospects and memories are indeed good company, however,

I am drawn, I am drawn,

he thought—

"toward I know not what. I feel life course through my body, yet I know being "in" this world is not enough."

He thought—

"My dues are paid; I have my ticket. Will I take flight?"

The transparency invites. Then…

he stopped thinking.

PURE BLUE SADNESS

Quietly rippled quilted flesh content
Upon a lawn of demure widows
Moving
          almost to adjust a tear.
Sprinting
          toward the denial of doom.
"Take me! Take me!"
"No, me!"
Occasions of silent wetness.
Booming victims of the compliant,
Tasting all the give and take,
They wrestle the past and forgotten
Memories.
Memories left to die.
Memories whose parents have been sold
To the master.
Memories silken and subtle
Against the firmness of all youth.
Grovel, but leave this present.
Tomorrow's tea does not invite.
Goodbye; Release.
Another chance, another view
Of pure blue sadness.

(FROM THE INSIDE) FREEDOM'S SONG

Pecking through
Some cocoons
        Some free within
Stake out limits
        Limits they will not cross
To freedom.
Barking from without,
Just beyond recognizable pale
Free from all
But frustration.
Barking at pecking begings
Both confined within concepts
Dictated by programmers invisible.

Light no longer a valid commodity
Understanding only packaged norms
Pecking and barking
Analyze the emptiness
Of others' analysis and
Never skip a beat in their
Dance of freedom
"And one and two."

MORNING SONG

The Sun,

Having not yet broken fast

Was up nonetheless

Making hurried preparations

For his part in the day.

Hurried

Because the birds

(Unable to hold it any longer)

Were bathing themselves,

each other

and the morning

in song.

The baby, you and I

Stir simultaneously.

I slowly become aware

Of my awareness

And dreams become reality.

Before the day's events

Call on me,

Offering me personal omnipotence

And public indifference

Wee moments are mine

To converse groggily with creation.

With you

Misty-eyed and soft,

Trusting our life together

By your restful sleep.

With our son,

His heart strong

And vision true

To the new sensations of his world,

I stretch,

And think of the sun's dewy radiance,

Of the wonders

The robin's song calls forth.

Remembering only vaguely the time,

I stretch again

Hesitate

And decide

Our table of joy

Needs one more spoon.

I like the robins

Very much

But I love you.

I like the robins

But I love you

Very much.

ICE AND ICE

Crying eyes out

ice out

toward the black-coaled

cold un-souled face

of the paper reaper

raper of multi-kinded

shredded smiles

down

the rain drain

of sane plain folk

celebrating cerebral freedom

from

omnipotent omni

ivy-eyed ignorant

verbally venomous vipers

leaning

toward passive

yet purposeful misunderstanding.

MILES' MUTED BLUES

Only if it's

focusing on one

on another,

holding an edge that

remains drinkable on

hot August nights...on the

muted blues of Miles,

and miles of dreams

of attending moments of

fear, loss of focus, sweet

sweet slide to the memories

of conversations with

yourself. Ice.

Bitchen'! Only if

it's...Sorry, your time is up.

FLOWER WISDOM

Beaten and worn by my culture

I sought to live with the flowers.

But they turned me away saying,

"You have a good heart but no courage."

"What can I do," I asked.

"Live among your own."

"I can't; I've tried. It's too hard."

"They need you," the beautiful flower said, "You need them.

Gain courage and shine whenever you can."

I thanked them and sadly walked home to feed the birds.

TINY VOICES

Where do we meet the tiny voices?

In our expectations or theirs? If ours, why

do we have the right to impose? If theirs,

do we learn? Do we respect? Do we evolve

by rote? Are we open to new, to others' ideas?

Do we even pay attention to our own tiny voices,

let alone others?

If we do not listen nor meet these voices,

we are doomed to repeat the madness. We are

doomed to hear only echoes.

CAN YOU HEAR ME?

Ten thousand lifetimes.

A dinosaur sound. Faint.

From an infinite remove

a tiny man winks, waves.

(From the right side of my heart

love streams) I wave back.

Swimming in the love

I cling to the tiny man.

He is me.

We embrace.

I take his hand

and enter his world.

RUTHIE'S DILEMMA

They looked like bird feet hanging off my legs. For a moment I became confused, frightened, then stressed. But after a while, remembering what they were there for, I proceeded to salt and pepper them, saute' them with a few shitake mushrooms and Vidalia onions. Boy did we have a feast! Later, my wife, Ruthie, asked me why I was walking so funny, and did I want her to cook up some liver for supper.

ESCAPED NORMALITY

To be

    visions

Lives lived in mountain snows

Languageless

Just close and

Enough

    is from never and never

Will free salutation

From sameness.

It never is—

We know it, admit (afterwards eyes

Dew

    surroundings, living silk removed

Again?

    And yes and forever yes)

Complicity.

Be strong…life and death are

Yet young.

Do not impose from without.

Enjoy.

We grow, we continue.

Till from a certain angle

We are no longer what we are.

GIVING BIRTH TO DEATH

There wasn't anyone there under the leaf when I looked the last time so I just took it for granted that she hadn't had them yet and actually I never even thought of it at 6:04 AM Monday June 23 when I went out into the fresh morning air, to inhale the dewy pungent breath from God's own mouth until the next morning at approximately the same time when I did remember to look at the frail, fragile crushed particles and slime that would have been a beautiful tiny bird.

ONE

Long-striding tiger people

carrying amber torches

slipped through an opening

in the dense night

in search of

the soft under-belly of dawn.

Their muscles taut

as they skated across the dewy courtyard.

And waving at me

in the picture frame window,

joyously stroked

their huge, blood gorged genitals

impregnating my view

with silver-winged

transparent butterflies

to flood my weary mind

with their invisible movies.

And as I watched their life flow

(no buttered popcorn

no fifty cent coke)

I observed my life and theirs,

each trying to learn

without interfering.

TWO

Without interfering

I secretly

sent a valentine

(long ago)

to a girl named Hilda.

Not quite sure

of my initial attraction,

but as I recall

she had very large

BREASTS.

She played the accordion.

No joke.

Not until later

when I became aware of

how I was expected to feel

about large breasts and accordions.

ch—ch—ch

THREE

changes

Did Peter Pain

ever go straight?

Or is he still love/hating

Ben Gay?

Peter Pain and Ben Gay.

They were such a nice couple.

The last time I saw them together

they were sitting silently,

holding memories,

watching the transparent butterfly movies.

Much much later,

after the event,

someone told me

they had gone their separate ways.

Don't hurt no more stuff

the current rage.

No empathy for painful deviance.

One day, some days, hurt was good.

The world focused more sharply.

But time goes by so fast.

FOUR

And good-bye,

wishing he'd not looked back

seeing her small and standing there.

And good-bye.

Transparent butterfly movie

reels backwards.

A voice on the phone,

a game played

but only well by one.

There was an owl

that took him away,

that future tiger person

("and I'll scratch her eyes out")

An owl without eyes?

Who…no matter

but after…

Slim hand on thigh slyly,

Growing alarm!

The player says, “Don’t worry

I won’t touch what’s not mine.”

Tight green toreador pants

from all who saw.

Tiny Mexican dancer

with enormous hair and long black eyes.

How do you like her?

Later a movie star,

but too late.

She played the game well

and lost. Sail away.

FIVE

Flashing to a small bedroom

in a large house

outside

inside

heavy-eyed innocence

snuggles under a mountain of blankets

Warm,

but enough freedom

to catch the icicle chill

that helps to raise anticipated goose bumps.

As off in the distance

across the river

a train whistles through the darkness.

And directly below

Jack Benny and Amos and Andy

uneventfully but gratefully

pass the eve to night

for the keepers of the innocence

till later

up the stairs and

"Our Father, who art in heaven."

The soft fluffy snow

made secret dancing sounds

as it lovingly teased the ground below.

Then magically was transformed

to crunch

under unsure, but kindly feet

heading home on this Winter's night.

SIX

Far away

the silent procession beckons

the orgasmic end and return

of now sleeping transparent butterflies

gently through the Mayan veil.

They again as in ages past mystically merge at closing time

into the tiger people's mission.

The priests to clean up the buttered popcorn

and fifty cent cokes

that never were.

Goodnight Hilda and Happy Valentines Day.

The closet is empty.

Ben and Peter off for a beer

then to bed

minding their own business.

Goodnight.

And good-bye.

Even looking back wisely

from this distant perspective,

she played the game well.

Innocence returns through rebirth of purpose.

It will always be and

always has been.

Life movies are over for the tiger people.

But eternally remain

again and again,

across the roads and neighborhoods of your soul.

Try to catch the show when it plays near you.

If it does.

I hope it does.

Printed in the United States
76505LV00006B/133-138

9 781424 168200